HONESTY

A missing key to unlock intimacy with God

A Compass – finances God's way™ book

To learn more about Compass
visit compass1.org

Dedication

To my wife, Lynn Dayton, who is the very
definition of *"A wife of noble character"*
(Proverbs 31:10).

She is the most honest and
caring person I know.

Acknowledgment

I am very grateful to Bill and Beth Neidlinger for opening their home to host the writing of this book.

To Brandon Sieben, Kyle Hasbrouck, Dan Schilling, Nick Breach, Andres Panasiuk, Bert Den Hertog, James Sims, Richard Samuel, Mario Denton, Timothy Manor, Paul Rahill, Tim Wright, and the entire Compass family – thank you for your hearts for Christ and commitment to help people from every nation learn God's way of handling money.

Designed by Dwayne Bassett of Sprocket Creative

Edited by Steve Gardner and Larry Libby

Unless otherwise indicated, all Scripture quotations are taken from the New American Standard Bible®, copyright © 1960, 1962, 1963, 1968, 1971, 1972, 1973, 1975, 1995 by the Lockman Foundation. Used by permission.

Scripture quotations marked NIV are taken from the Holy Bible, *New International Version, NIV.* Copyright © 1973, 1978, 1984, 2011 by Biblica, Inc.® (Some quotations may be from the earlier NIV edition, copyright 1984.) Used by permission. All rights reserved worldwide.

ISBN 978-1-7348223-3-5

TABLE OF CONTENTS

CHAPTER ONE

Honesty Is Essential

Each of us, whether we realize it or not, make dozens of decisions every day of our lives that tell a story about our honesty.

Do I tell the cashier at the store when I receive too much change?

Do I tell this person the WHOLE truth about what I'm trying to sell them?

Do I commit to a task knowing deep down that I probably won't follow through?

Making the right decisions and keeping our word are even more difficult when everyone around us seems to be shading the truth and fudging on their commitments. Judges 17:6 described a similar period in Israel's history. The writer summed up his generation—and the whole nation—with the words: *"Every man did what was right in his own eyes."* It's really no different today. People formulate their own standards of honesty, which change depending upon their circumstances.

Early in his career, a man I know (we'll call him John Brady) developed a pattern of dishonesty. He underreported income to diminish taxes, lied to insurance companies to save money on premiums, subtly cheated his employees and customers, and advertised promises his business could never hope to deliver. John's only goal in life was to become as rich as he could as quickly as he could—and he really didn't care how he did it or whom he harmed in the process.

John's habit of dishonesty tainted all of his relationships—family, friends, and acquaintances. As time went by, a growing number of people recognized that he was not a man of integrity.

Full confession: I was that young man!

All that began to change when Jim Seneff, a close friend, asked me to join him in a study of the Bible to discover what it said about money. Carefully reading through the pages of Scripture, we eventually identified 2,350 verses related to money and possessions. As we arranged these passages topic by topic, I was stunned to see those ancient words flame into life. How could a book written thousands of years ago be so *practical*—so immediately applicable to so many contemporary struggles and problems?

Neither of us was ever the same after that study. And that's the truth. Learning and applying these principles had a profound—and permanent—impact on our personal finances and careers. Speaking for myself, that deep dive into God's Word changed the course of my whole life, especially in the area of honesty.

There are more than 400 verses in the Bible that communicate the Lord's desire for us to be completely honest. This is but a small sample:

- *"You shall not steal, nor deal falsely, nor lie to one another"* (Leviticus 19:11).

- *"Lying lips are an **abomination** to the Lord"* (Proverbs 12:22, emphasis added).

- *"The Lord **hates** . . . a lying tongue"* (Proverbs 6:16–17, emphasis added).

- *"The Lord **loathes** all cheating and dishonesty"* (Proverbs 20:23, TLB, emphasis added).

- *"You must have accurate and honest weights and measures, so that you may live long in the land the Lord your God is giving you. For the Lord your God **detests** anyone . . . who deals dishonestly"* (Deuteronomy 25:15–16, NIV, emphasis added).

- *"Therefore each of you must put off falsehood and speak truthfully to your neighbor, for we are all members of one body"* (Ephesians 4:25, NIV).

Carefully review these verses again. How does God feel about those who are dishonest? What is His requirement for honesty?

The God of Truth

Truthfulness is one of God's attributes. He is repeatedly identified as the God of truth. *"I, the* Lord, *speak the truth; I declare what is right"* (Isaiah 45:19, NIV). *"But when he, the* [Holy] *Spirit of truth, comes, he will guide you into all the truth . . ."* (John 16:13, NIV). In one powerful passage, Jesus declares that He is the very personification of truth. *"I am the way and the truth and the life. No one comes to the Father except through me"* (John 14:6, NIV).

The Lord commands us to reflect His honest and holy character: *". . . be holy yourselves also in all your behavior; because it is written, 'You shall be holy, for I* [the Lord] *am holy'"* (1 Peter 1:15-16).

God's nature is in stark contrast to Satan's. John 8:44 minces no words describing the devil's essential character: *". . . He was a murderer from the beginning, and does not stand in the truth because there is no truth in him. Whenever he speaks a lie, he speaks from his own nature, for he is a liar and the father of lies."* The Lord wants us to become conformed to His honest character rather than to the dishonest nature of the devil.

Take a moment to study this comparison between what the Scriptures teach and what our society generally practices concerning honesty.

Issue	Scripture	Society
Standard of honesty:	Total honesty	Partial honesty
God's concern about honesty:	He requires honesty	There is no God
Decision whether to be honest is based upon:	Faith in the invisible, living God	Only what I can see; risk vs. reward
Question often asked when deciding whether to be honest:	Will it please God?	Will I get away with it?

Honesty is Rare—and Important to God

We tend to underestimate how significant honesty is to the Lord. Jeremiah 5:1 says, *"Go up and down the streets of Jerusalem, look around and consider, search through her squares. If you can find but one person who deals honestly and seeks the truth, I will forgive this city"* (NIV).

Just think of it! The future of an entire city hung in the balance, and what was the Lord looking for before executing judgment on it? *Just one honest person!* The Lord is still looking for honest people. Are you willing to be that one person in your family, work, or community? If you are that individual, you may not be noticed by other people, but you will please an audience of One, the One who really matters—the Lord Jesus Christ.

CHAPTER TWO

Why God Requires Honesty

As you will discover through the pages of this book, the primary reason the Lord wants you and me to be honest is when we are truthful, we have the opportunity to enter into a closer, more intimate relationship with Christ. The flip side is also true. When we act dishonestly, our intimacy with Him is damaged.

Have you ever thought about this? When we are dishonest, we are acting as if the living God doesn't even exist! In essence, we decide that He isn't able to provide exactly what we need when we need it, even though He has promised to do so: *"My God shall supply all your needs according to His riches in glory in Christ Jesus"* (Philippians 4:19).

When we choose to take things into our own hands and do them our own dishonest way, we act as if God is incapable of discovering our dishonesty, and is powerless to discipline us. If we *really* believe God will discipline us, then we will not consider acting dishonestly.

Honest behavior is an issue of faith.

Have you ever thought of it in those terms?

An honest decision may look foolish in light of what we can see, but the godly person knows Jesus Christ is alive, even though invisible to us. Every honest decision strengthens our faith in the living God and helps us grow into a closer relationship with Christ.

If, however, we deliberately choose to be dishonest, we essentially deny our Lord and violate the greatest commandment: *"You shall love the Lord your God with all your heart, and with all your soul, and with all your mind"* (Matthew 22:37). It is impossible to love God like this if, at the same time, we are knowingly dishonest and behave as if He didn't even exist. It's as if we are practicing atheists.

When God gave the Ten Commandments, two of them specifically addressed honesty. *"You shall not steal"* (Exodus 20:15). *"You shall not bear false witness against your neighbor"* (Exodus 20:16). Jesus later told us, *"If you love Me, you* will *keep My commandments"* (John 14:15).

Think about this for a moment: If we disobey the Lord by practicing dishonesty, we cannot simultaneously love Him. In fact (and this one may shock you), Scripture declares that the dishonest actually hate God. *"He who walks in his uprightness fears the Lord, but he who is crooked in his ways despises Him"* (Proverbs 14:2).

We Cannot Practice Dishonesty and Love People

The Lord also requires honesty for another significant reason. Dishonest behavior violates the second great commandment, *"You shall love your neighbor as yourself"* (Mark 12:31). Romans 13:9–10 reads, *"If you love your neighbor as much as you love yourself you will not want to harm or cheat him, or kill him or steal from him . . . love does no wrong to anyone"* (TLB).

We should understand that when we act dishonestly for financial gain, it really amounts to stealing from another person. We may deceive ourselves into thinking that it's a business or the government or an insurance company suffering the loss. But if we look at the bottom line, it is the business owners or fellow taxpayers or policy holders from whom we are stealing.

It's just as if we took the money from their wallets.

Financial dishonesty always injures people.

The victim is always a *person.*

Honesty Creates Credibility for Evangelism

Our Lord also desires total honesty to enable us to demonstrate the reality of Jesus Christ to those who don't yet know Him.

I will never forget the first time I told a neighbor how he could come to know Christ as his personal Savior. In a flash of anger, he snarled, "Well, I know a businessman who always goes to church and talks a lot about Jesus, but watch out if you ever get in a business deal with him! He'd cheat his own grandmother! If that's what it means to be a Christian, I don't want any part of it!"

Our actions speak so much louder than our words. Scripture says to *"prove yourselves to be blameless and innocent, children of God above reproach in the midst of a crooked and perverse generation, among whom you appear as lights in the world"* (Philippians 2:15).

We can influence people *for* Christ by our honesty. Robert Newsom had been trying to sell an antique pickup truck for months. Finally, an interested buyer decided to make the purchase. At the last minute, however, the buyer said, "Listen. I'll buy this truck on one condition. I don't want you to report this sale, so I won't have to pay state sales tax."

Although strongly tempted to comply with this last-second demand, Robert responded, "I'm sorry, I can't do that because Jesus Christ is my Lord." Robert later said, "You should have witnessed the buyer's reaction. He almost went into shock! Then an interesting thing happened. His attitude completely changed. Not only did he purchase the truck, but he eagerly joined my wife and me around our dinner table. Rarely have I seen anyone as open to the truth about knowing Christ in a personal way."

That's the premise of this whole book.

Honesty opens doors of intimacy to God and the people we rub shoulders with every day. Because Robert acted honestly even though it was going to cost him money (*"Prove yourselves to be blameless and innocent, children of God above reproach"*), he demonstrated to this person (*"a crooked and perverse generation"*) the reality of a personal faith in Jesus Christ (*"appear as lights in the world"*).

Here's another way to say it: If we claim to serve a Holy God but our behavior doesn't confirm this, it creates a disconnect for those who don't yet know Christ. As we read earlier, 1 Peter 1:15–16 tells us, "*. . . be holy yourselves also in all your behavior; because it is written, 'You shall be holy, for I am holy.'*"

We are to be salt and light to those around us, and one of the most practical and effective ways of doing this is with a fresh determination to be honest.

Small things are small things, but faithfulness with a small thing is a big thing. – Hudson Taylor

Honesty Helps Confirm God's Direction

Proverbs 4:24-26 says, *"Put away from you a deceitful mouth, and put devious speech far from you. Let your eyes look directly ahead, and let your gaze be fixed straight in front of you. Watch the path of your feet and* **all your ways will be established"** (emphasis added).

What a tremendous principle! As you are completely honest, *"all your ways will be established."* Choosing to walk the narrow path of honesty eliminates the many possible avenues of dishonesty. Decision making becomes simpler because the honest path is a clearer path. From time to time we all struggle with major decisions. What vocation should I pursue? Should I marry this person? Which vehicle or home should I buy? Honesty helps confirm God's direction in decisions.

"If only I had understood this," Raymond wept. "But Donna and I wanted that home so much. It was our dream house. But our debts! We were so far in the hole that we couldn't qualify for the mortgage. The only way for us to buy the house was to conceal some of our debts from the lender.

"It was the worst decision of our lives. Almost immediately, we were unable to meet the mortgage payment and pay our other debts, too. The pressure built and was almost more than Donna could stand. Our dream house ended up causing a family nightmare. I lost not only the home but nearly lost my wife."

Had Raymond and Donna been honest, if they had told the simple truth, the lender would not have approved the loan. They would not have been able to purchase that particular home. Had they prayed, waited, and focused on paying off some of their current debt, perhaps the Lord would have brought something more affordable or an opportunity beyond their expectations. They would have avoided the pressure—the agonizing, arguing, and tears—that almost ended their marriage. Honesty helps confirm God's direction.

My former business was real estate development. In some cases, several years would elapse between the inception of a project and its completion. As we all know, our nation's economy can change radically during that time. What might appear to be a sensible project in the beginning could become a disaster. I was afraid of launching a project if the Lord didn't want me to build. When considering a new development, I would pray, "Lord, show me clearly if You want me involved, but slam the door shut if You don't." I wanted to be certain that it was really God who was providing that opportunity. And how could I know if God was shutting a door to protect me if I forced it open through dishonesty?

Honesty in Small Things

The Lord requires us to be honest even in small matters. *"Whoever can be trusted with very little can also be trusted with much, and whoever is dishonest with very little will also be dishonest with much"* (Luke 16:10, NIV).

I know through personal experience.

My wife, Lynn, had an urgent need for an item that she asked me to purchase when I went to town to meet a friend. Unfortunately, I completely forgot about it. Several hours later I was almost home when she called to confirm the purchase.

I was embarrassed. I panicked. I lied.

"The store had sold out of the item," I told her. She had more questions, and I answered with more lies. It was so absurd! I kept getting in deeper and deeper over something so small. The closer I got to home, the more ashamed I felt. As soon as I walked through the front door I told her the truth and asked for her forgiveness, which she generously granted.

Small lies are a slippery slope that damage our character and inevitably lead to greater dishonesty. The reverse is also true. When we are honest in small matters, we are much more likely to be honest when the stakes are larger.

Missionary pioneer Hudson Taylor said it this way, "Small things are small things, but faithfulness with a small thing is a big thing."

CHAPTER THREE

Escaping the Temptation of Dishonesty

Let's face it, from time to time we are all are tempted to be dishonest.

Thankfully, several practical steps can help us overcome these temptations.

Nurture a Healthy Fear of the Lord

When I talk of a "healthy fear" of the Lord, I don't mean thinking of God as a big celestial bully with a club, just waiting for the opportunity to whack us back in line. No, He is a loving Father who, out of infinite love, disciplines His children for their benefit. *"... He disciplines us for our good, so that we may share His holiness"* (Hebrews 12:10).

Hebrews 12:11 tells us, *"All discipline for the moment seems not to be joyful, but sorrowful."* Discipline hurts! Given the choice, I would much prefer to "share His holiness" out of obedience to His Word rather than make a deliberate decision that prompts my loving Father to discipline me.

What's more, I believe our heavenly Father will not allow us to keep anything we have acquired dishonestly. Proverbs 13:11 reads, *"Wealth obtained by fraud dwindles."*

A friend told the following experience to me. She had purchased four azalea plants, but the check-out clerk had charged her for only one.

She knew it, but left the store anyway without paying for the other three. She went on to say it was simply miraculous how quickly three of those azalea plants shriveled up and died—and the fourth wasn't doing too well, either!

Think about this for a moment: If you are a parent and one of your children steals something, do you allow the child to keep it? Of course not! You require its return because the child's character would be damaged if he kept stolen property. Not only do you insist on its return, but you usually want the child to experience enough discomfort to produce a lasting impression. For instance, you might have the child confess the theft and ask forgiveness from the store manager. When our heavenly Father lovingly disciplines us, it is usually done in such a way that we won't soon forget.

Proverbs 16:6 summarizes the benefit of this healthy fear: *"By the fear of the Lord one keeps away from evil."*

Distance Yourself from the Dishonest

Scripture teaches that we are deeply influenced by those around us, either for good or evil. David recognized this and said, *"My eyes shall be upon the faithful of the land, that they may dwell with me; he who walks in a blameless way is the one who will minister to me. He who practices deceit shall not dwell within my house; he who speaks falsehood shall not maintain his position before me"* (Psalm 101:6–7).

Paul wrote, *"Do not be deceived: 'Bad company corrupts good morals'"* (1 Corinthians 15:33). Solomon was even stronger: *"He who is a partner with a thief hates his own life"* (Proverbs 29:24).

Obviously, we can't isolate ourselves from everyone who is dishonest. If that were the case, how could followers of Christ become salt and light in our world? Even so, we should be very discerning about those with whom we closely associate.

If I observe a person who is dishonest in his dealings with the government or in a small matter, I know this person will be dishonest in greater matters—and probably in his dealings with me. In my opinion, it is impossible for a person to be *selectively* honest. Either an individual has made the commitment to be absolutely honest, or his dishonesty will become more prevalent. Those around him will be tempted to follow his example. It is much easier to remain completely honest if you are surrounded by others who are of a like mind and conviction.

Practice the Golden Rule

"Do not merely look out for your own personal interests but also for the interests of others" (Philippians 2:4). This verse is better translated, "look intently" after the interests of others. The Lord challenged me with this passage, and pointed out my self-centeredness and lack of concern for others. And He did it just as I was about to purchase some land.

This particular seller wasn't represented by a broker—and had virtually no experience in real estate. He knew nothing of its value. I had communicated to the seller that my modest offer reflected its true market value, but I was secretly congratulating myself. I knew very well that the purchase price I had offered was much too low. Not once had I given any thought about the interests of the seller. Not once had I even considered what would be fair to him. I had concentrated solely on acquiring the property at the lowest possible price.

Over the next few hours, however, I found myself reexamining the transaction in the light of "looking intently" after the seller's interests as well as my own. I concluded that I should pay more for the property to reflect its true value. Practicing the Golden Rule is sometimes costly, but its reward is a clear conscience before the Lord and people.

> *The mind is where all integrity begins, an intentional decision that nothing will compromise my commitment to be honest. Even if I stand alone. No matter what others around me do.*

Give Generously

Giving generously to those in need helps us escape the temptation of acting dishonestly. *"He who steals must steal no longer; but rather he must labor, performing with his own hands what is good so that he will have something to share with one who has need"* (Ephesians 4:28).

As we give, it draws us closer to Christ and reduces our incentive to steal. After all, if we're going to give something away, there's not much reason to steal it!

Walk by the Spirit

A friend was teaching these principles of honesty to a class in a secular college. One student raised his hand and said, "I think we all would like to be the honest person you're talking about." He paused, then added, "But I know if the right opportunity comes along, I'm going to be dishonest." At least that student was being honest about his dishonesty! Apart from denying ourselves and living lives yielded to the Holy Spirit, all of us will be dishonest.

Galatians 5:16–17 says it this way: *"Walk by the Spirit, and you will not gratify the desires of the sinful nature. For the sinful nature desires what is contrary to the Spirit, and the Spirit what is contrary to the sinful nature"* (NIV).

Let's face it, the desire—the bent—of our human nature is to act dishonestly. You might say that deceit is the natural default for all men and women. Scripture tells that *"from within, out of men's hearts, come evil thoughts . . . theft . . . deceit"* (Mark 7:21–22, NIV). In sharp contrast, the desire of the Spirit is for us to be totally honest. I can't overemphasize that the completely honest life is supernatural. For all our good intentions, we can't achieve this on our own. We must submit ourselves entirely to Jesus Christ as Lord and invite Him to live His life through us. There is no other way.

This is especially true for those who are people pleasers, because they want everyone to like them. Instinctively, they shy away from speaking difficult truths, not wanting to deliver what they consider bad news to someone's face.

They are often inclined to convey only what they think others want to hear, whether it is true or not.

Thankfully, 2 Timothy 1:7 points the way for people pleasers to replace their fear by becoming courageous truth tellers: "*For the Spirit God gave us does not make us timid, but gives us power, love and self-discipline*" (NIV, emphasis added). In other words, when we submit to the Holy Spirit, His power transforms our timidity into courage.

Ask Yourself Why

people Pleasing

When you are tempted to be dishonest, train yourself to ask a simple question: Why am I inclined to be dishonest in this situation? Your motivation may be readily apparent to you, or you may need to pray and reflect until it becomes clear.

Some of the most common reasons are: fear, lack of trusting God, greed, coveting, impatience, jealousy, embarrassment, and disliking another person.

For example, can you remember an instance when you tried to help God solve one of your problems by being dishonest? You may have reasoned, *God must not realize what a terrible predicament I'm facing! If He did, He would have provided me the solution already. I'd better solve the problem right now in my own way.* In this example, the motivations probably would have been impatience and lack of trusting God.

Once you recognize what is influencing you to be dishonest, ask these questions: Does this please the Lord? What would Jesus do?

Cultural Influences

The most difficult of temptations to recognize and overcome are what I call "cultural temptations" or "cultural assumptions." These occur when it seems like everyone around us is doing it. These cultural temptations are so pervasive that we may not ever recognize them as unbiblical—until we take the time to measure them against God's Word.

Cultural temptations occur in groups as small as families or friends, or as large as communities, governments, and even entire countries. These groups often exert strong peer pressure to conform and practice corruption, lying, or stealing. It's not only accepted by the group, it is *expected.*

It's not easy taking a stand for what is *right* when everyone around you is running after what is *wrong.* It's not easy swimming against the strong riptide of public opinion. Jesus Himself warned us that *"small is the gate and narrow the road that leads to life, and only a few find it"* (Matthew 7:14, NIV).

Overcoming Cultural Temptations

As a teenager, Daniel was captured in Jerusalem as a prisoner of war and transplanted in Babylon. He was given a new name that referred to one of the Babylonian's many gods. Then he entered a rigorous three-year training program to learn the Babylonian language, literature, lifestyle, and religion—all designed to brainwash Daniel into turning away from following the one true God. The peer pressure around him was suffocating. And beyond that, refusal to fall in line with Babylon's reeducation project could have meant a death sentence.

And Daniel didn't have to wait long for the moment of truth. When he and his companions were offered provisions from the king's table (which had probably been sacrificed to idols), he *"made up his mind that he would not defile himself with the king's choice food"* (Daniel 1:8). The mind is where all integrity begins, an intentional decision that nothing will compromise my commitment to be honest.

Even if I stand alone.

Even if I am rejected.

Even if it kills me.

No matter what others around me do. Regardless of the circumstances or the extent of the peer pressure, I will be a truthful person. Daniel made this commitment as a teenager and maintained it his entire life.

Prayerfully answer this question: are you willing to make that commitment?

CHAPTER FOUR

What to Do When Dishonest

As we have said, from time to time, many of us—even the best of us—will be dishonest. What then? What should we do once we recognize that we have acted in a deceitful way? I'd like to suggest three steps to reestablish our relationship with the Lord and the people involved.

Remember, intimacy with Christ and a closer relationship with others are the primary purposes for God's requirement for honesty. He wants us to take these steps for our benefit and the benefit of those with whom we have been dishonest.

Restore Fellowship with God

Anytime we act dishonestly, we sin and break our fellowship with our Lord. This needs to be restored. First John 1:9 tells us how: *"If we confess our sins, He is faithful and righteous to forgive us our sins and to cleanse us from all unrighteousness."*

We must agree with God that our dishonesty was sin: that is confession. Then we thankfully accept God's gracious forgiveness so we can again enjoy His fellowship.

In the wake of such a prayer, it may still be difficult for you to believe or feel that your dishonesty was forgiven by the Lord. Regrets and self-incrimination may linger. This is the time to trust God and His word. If He says you have been forgiven, it is literally true—whether you feel like it or not. Psalm 103:12 tells us that *"As far as the east is from the west, so far has He* [the Lord] *removed our transgressions from us."*

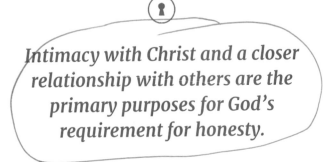

Intimacy with Christ and a closer relationship with others are the primary purposes for God's requirement for honesty.

Restore Fellowship with the Offended Person

After our fellowship with Christ has been restored, we need to confess our dishonesty to the person we offended. The apostle James tells us, *"Confess your sins to one another"* (James 5:16).

Ouch!

Really, James? This hurts!

I've had only a handful of people confess that they have wronged me. Interestingly, some of these people are now among my closest friends, in part, because of my respect for them. They so desired an honest relationship with me that they were willing to expose their sins.

Confessing to others was extremely difficult for me because of my pride. I'll never forget
the first time. Sweaty palms, dry throat and all,
I needed to confess my sin of lying to another
person . . . not that I hadn't had plenty of opportunities before!

He responded with a range of emotions: ini-
tial surprise, disappointment in me, and finally,
gratitude that I wanted to make things right.

Afterward I sensed a wonderful freedom in
our relationship. I also discovered that confession
helps break the habit of dishonesty because it is a
painfully humbling experience.

A person's lack of financial health may be a
consequence of violating this principle. *"He who
conceals his transgressions will not prosper, but he
who confesses and forsakes them will find compas-
sion"* (Proverbs 28:13).

Restore any Dishonestly Acquired Property

Finally, if we have acquired anything dishonestly,
we must return it to its rightful owner. *"Then it
shall be, when he sins and becomes guilty, that he shall
restore what he took by robbery . . . or anything about
which he swore falsely; he shall make restitution for it
in full and add to it one-fifth more. He shall give it to
the one to whom it belongs"* (Leviticus 6:4-5).

Restitution is a tangible effort to correct a wrong. Zacchaeus, the famously pint-sized tax collector in the gospel of Luke, is an example of fulfilling this principle. He promised Jesus, *"If I have defrauded anyone of anything, I will give back four times as much"* (Luke 19:8).

If it's not possible for restitution to be made to the injured party, then the property should be given to the Lord. Numbers 5:8 teaches, *"But if the man has no relative to whom restitution may be made for the wrong, the restitution which is made for the wrong must go to the Lord for the priest."*

Repentance: A Change of Mind and Heart

Restoring your close fellowship with Christ and others is God's primary objective, but He also wants you to experience repentance, which simply means a change of mind and heart concerning dishonesty.

In Luke chapter 3, John the Baptist powerfully warned those coming to be baptized by him to repent of their misdeeds. Three groups of people—the crowd, tax collectors, and soldiers—asked the identical question: "What should we do?" Interestingly, the answers to two of the groups had to do with honesty.

- John told the tax collectors, *"Don't collect any more than you are required to"* (Luke 3:13, NIV).

- John replied to the soldiers, *"Don't extort money and don't accuse people falsely"* (Luke 3:14, NIV).

Remember, the Lord hungers for the closest possible fellowship with you. With that reality firmly in mind, I encourage you to ask the Lord the same question right now. "What should I do? What should I do to please You by becoming a totally honest person?"

Key
Posture of the heart

CHAPTER FIVE

Forgive the Dishonest

Imagine you are a teenager, deeply loved by your father. Your jealous siblings sell you into slavery and lie to your father, claiming you were killed by a wild animal.

For more than a decade you are a slave and a prisoner in a foreign country. Amazingly, on one unbelievable day, you find yourself elevated to second in command of the world's most powerful nation. Several years later, your starving siblings—the very ones who betrayed and sold you—beg you for food. What's your response: retaliation or forgiveness?

This is the real-life question Joseph had to answer.

And he decided to forgive them.

How? How was he able to do this? Because he recognized that God had orchestrated his circumstances—even the ones that were so deeply traumatic and painful. *"God sent me ahead of you . . ."* he told his brothers, *"to save your lives by a great deliverance. So then, it was not you who sent me here, but God"* (Genesis 45:7-8, NIV).

God realizes how critical it is for us to forgive those who have caused or contributed to our loss or pain, regardless of their motivation. One of the most impressive characteristics of Jesus Christ was His willingness to forgive. Imagine hanging on a cross in unspeakable agony and at the same time praying for those who had crucified you: *"Father, forgive them; for they do not know what they are doing"* (Luke 23:34).

When the apostle Peter asked Jesus if he should forgive someone seven times, He responded, *"not seven times, but seventy-seven times"* (Matthew 18:22, NIV). He then told a parable about a servant who was forgiven a massive debt by his master—but stubbornly refused to forgive a fellow servant a trivial debt. Christ describes what happens to the unforgiving servant: *"In anger his master turned him over to the jailers to be tortured, until he should pay back all he owed. This is how my heavenly Father will treat each of you unless you forgive your brother from your heart"* (Matthew 18:34, NIV).

"Be kind and compassionate to one another, forgiving each other, just as in Christ God forgave you."

(Ephesians 4:32, NIV).

In order to grow more like Christ and experience the benefits He intends for us when we are the victim of dishonesty, we must forgive.

And more than forgive, we are to be kind, compassionate, and seek to be a blessing. *"Be kind and compassionate to one another, forgiving each other, just as in Christ God forgave you* (Ephesians 4:32, NIV). *"Not returning evil for evil or insult for insult, but giving a blessing instead; for you were called for the very purpose that you might inherit a blessing"* (1 Peter 3:9).

Unforgiveness can be a daily battle, particularly if the situation has been horribly hurtful. But if allowed to fester in the memory and emotions, it deeply harms the person who refuses to forgive. A friend described it as swallowing poison and hoping the other person will die. When we refuse to forgive, the bitterness in our heart can turn toxic, consuming our thoughts and eating away our emotional health. Forgiveness and seeking to bless the other person, however—as counter-intuitive as that might seem—leads to freedom, even joy.

It is imperative to pray regularly for the Lord to give us the desire to forgive, and then to give us His love for the people who may have harmed us. Jesus tells us also to pray *enemies and pray for those wh you may be sons of your Father* (Matthew 5:44). It's hard to someone for whom you are p

More than Forgiveness

Dave Johnstone was speechless. It was as if a high-voltage electrical shock had jolted him.

Scott, the Chairman of the Board, unexpectedly informed Dave that he was no longer employed at the company, effective immediately. When Dave questioned Scott about the reasons for termination, Scott reacted angrily and told him that three other executives had met with the Board and given them an ultimatum: fire Dave or they would resign.

"But this makes no sense," Dave responded in bewilderment. "Our market share is at an all-time high, we're financially healthy, and we have great new software under development." But Scott flatly refused to discuss it further.

Dave was the founder and CEO of a highly successful software company that he had started in his garage a quarter of a century earlier. Dave had been generous to reward the work of others by giving so much of his company's stock to the Board of Directors and leadership team that they now owned a majority of the stock and were in control.

Dave had been grooming three executives as possible successor, and he had chosen to be ss than any of them. Later, Dave learned that they had become impatient waiting for him to retire, so they conspired with the Chairman to fire him.

Devastated, Dave took a year to recover. Then he started a new software company. Although he made a commitment not to initiate recruitment of his former company's employees, some approached him because its culture had changed dramatically after his departure. Dave's new business grew steadily.

In less than a decade, his former company's revenues shriveled to only twenty percent of what they had been when Dave was fired, and it was close to going out of business. Their largest customer was dissatisfied with the performance of their most recent software and asked Dave to become their software provider.

Dave had forgiven Scott and the leadership and prayed often for them. He felt that God wanted him to help Scott, so he had his software engineers analyze the deficient software. They discovered how it could be improved. Dave called Scott and told him that he would help improve their software so that they could hold onto their remaining customer base.

Crazy Christianity! That's what some would say. Others would add, "Insanity! What about greater market share and putting your ruthless competitor out of business? What about the bottom line?"

By now you may be thinking, *Where did Dave learn to manage his business?* Dave's decisions to first forgive and then assist his former company are based on what the Bible teaches.[1]

CHAPTER SIX

Honesty in Leaders

The Lord is especially concerned with the honesty of men and women in positions of leadership, because of the *influence* these leaders have with their subordinates. The owner of a trucking company began wearing cowboy boots to work. Within six months, all the men in his office were in boots. When the owner suddenly changed back to a traditional business shoe, all the men were wearing business shoes within six months.

In a similar way, a dishonest leader produces dishonest followers. *"If a ruler pays attention to falsehood, all his ministers become wicked"* (Proverbs 29:12). Leaders must set the example of honesty in their personal and professional lives before they can expect those under their authority to do the same. I believe a leader should be careful to *"abstain from all **appearance** of evil"* (1 Thessalonians 5:22, KJV, emphasis added). Why? Because if a leader's honest actions are construed as dishonest, that perception will exert a powerful influence on others, because even a leader's actions that are honest but interpreted as dishonest deeply influence others.

The president of an international construction company was once asked why his company declined to work in countries where bribes and graft were a way of life. He replied, with wisdom, "We never build in those countries, no matter how profitable the project may appear, because we can't afford to. If my staff believes we are acting dishonestly, they will eventually become thieves. Their dishonesty will ultimately cost us more than we could ever earn on a project."

Selection of Leaders

Dishonesty should disqualify a person from leadership. Listen to the counsel of Jethro, Moses' father-in-law: *"You shall select out of all the people able men who fear God, men of truth, those who hate dishonest gain; and you shall place these . . . as leaders of thousands, of hundreds, of fifties, and of tens"* (Exodus 18:21). These leaders were not only to avoid dishonest gain—they were to hate it!

Two of the four criteria for leadership selection that Jethro gave Moses dealt with honesty: *"men of truth, those who hate dishonest gain."* I believe the Lord wants us to continue to select leaders on the basis of these same character qualities.

Integrity should be the key that unlocks the door of considering someone to serve as a leader. No matter how capable or experienced or charismatic their personality, if a person lacks integrity they should not be invited to lead.

Preservation of Leaders

Not only are leaders selected, in part, by honest behavior, but a leader retains his position by honest behavior. *"A leader . . . who hates unjust gain will prolong his days"* (Proverbs 28:16). *"Loyalty and truth preserve the king, and he upholds his throne by righteousness"* (Proverbs 20:28).

We have all witnessed leaders who have been demoted or dismissed because of a root problem of personal corruption. The prophet Jeremiah confronted King Jehoiakim with these scathing words *". . . Did not your father* [King Josiah] *eat and drink and do justice and righteousness? . . . Then it was well. Is not that what it means to know Me?"* declares the LORD.

"But your eyes and your heart are intent **only upon your own dishonest gain**, *and on shedding innocent blood and on practicing oppression and extortion. Therefore thus says the* LORD *in regard to Jehoiakim the son of Josiah, king of Judah . . . He will be buried with a donkey's burial, dragged off and thrown out beyond the gates of Jerusalem"* (Jeremiah 22:15–19, emphasis added).

Accountability

How can a leader maintain the standard of complete honesty and not compromise his or her integrity?

Allow me to suggest the answer in a single, powerful word: *accountability.* A leader who takes this crucial precaution seriously must establish a system of checks and balances to ensure that he or she is accountable to a trusted friend or colleague—or several of them. The purpose, of course, isn't to usurp the leader's authority, but rather provide a workable structure for this safeguard.

Bribes

A bribe is anything given to influence a person to do something illegal or wrong. The taking of bribes is clearly prohibited in the Bible: *"You shall not take a bribe, for a bribe blinds the clear-sighted and subverts the cause of the just"* (Exodus 23:8). If a leader takes bribes, it may jeopardize the business or governing body. Proverbs 29:4 says it this way, *"The king gives stability to the land by justice, but a man who takes bribes overthrows it."*

Government

Corruption in governments around the world is common many places, characterized by bribes, kickbacks, and stealing by officials. An extreme example was the community of Bell, California, with a population of 35,000. Comprised mostly of lower-income working families, elected officials were convicted of misappropriating public funds through exorbitant salaries, benefits, and illicit loans of public money. Its city manager was paid a salary of $787,000—or nearly twice that of the President of the United States.

Leaders at every level of government are required by the Lord to be personally honest. In addition, they need to create an environment of honesty in their jurisdiction. They build this culture by rescuing victims of dishonesty and by demanding that all government workers conduct themselves above reproach. When they discover a corrupt public servant, they should quickly terminate the offender and strongly consider prosecution to warn others.

Jeremiah 21:11–12 captures how seriously God views this responsibility. *"Say to the royal house of Judah, 'Hear the word of the Lord . . . Administer justice every morning; rescue from the hand of the oppressor the one who has been robbed, or my wrath will break out and burn like fire because of the evil you have done—burn with no one to quench it.'"*

The Bible shines a bright spotlight on the actions of corrupt government officials. You might say its pages are littered with them. Here is a small sample:

- *". . . they* [leaders of Jerusalem] *are shepherds who have no understanding; they have all turned to their own way, each one to his unjust gain, to the last one"* (Isaiah 56:11).

- "*Her princes within* [Israel] *are like wolves tearing the prey, by shedding blood and destroying lives in order to get dishonest gain . . . The people of the land have practiced oppression and committed robbery*" (**Ezekiel 22:27, 29**).

Integrity should be the key that unlocks the door of considering someone to serve as a leader.

Daniel and the Lions' Den

Daniel is well known for his God-given gift of interpreting dreams and visions—some of which unfolded the world's history from his day to far into the future. Even more impressive, however, is Daniel's performance as a government official. Throughout his years of service to foreign kings in a distant land, Daniel's character and integrity in office were nothing less than magnificent.

After King Darius the Mede defeated the Babylonian kingdom, he appointed 120 officials to rule the kingdom, and three administrators to whom the officials were accountable. Daniel so distinguished himself by his exceptional qualities that the king planned to elevate him to prime minister. This infuriated the other officials.

"*At this, the administrators and [officials] tried to find grounds for charges against Daniel in his conduct of government affairs, but they were unable to do so. They could find no evidence of corruption in him, because he was trustworthy and neither corrupt nor negligent*" (Daniel 6:4, NIV, emphasis added).

Knowing Daniel's devotion to God, they appealed to King Darius's vanity by asking him to adopt a law requiring everyone to pray to the king alone, or to be tossed into the lion's den. Despite the threatened consequences, however, Daniel continued praying to the Lord—on schedule and in the open—and was thrown into the lions' den.

The Lord saved him from certain death, and Daniel responded to the king: "*My God sent His angel and shut the lions' mouths and they have not harmed me, inasmuch as I was found innocent before Him; and also toward you, O king, I have committed no crime*" (Daniel 6:22).

Here is a question for all who serve in government: Are you committed to discharge your duties with complete integrity like Daniel . . . no matter what?

Taxes

What does the Bible say about paying taxes? That's the same question that was asked of Jesus. *"Is it lawful for us to pay taxes to Caesar or not? . . . [Jesus] said to them, 'Show Me a [Roman coin]. Whose likeness and inscription does it have?' They said, 'Caesar's.' And He said to them, 'Then render [give] to Caesar the things that are Caesar's, and to God what is God's'"* (Luke 20:22–25).

Some people will tell you to avoid paying taxes at any cost. After all, they will reason, look how much the government wastes and squanders. Even so, the Bible tells us to pay our taxes. *"Every person is to be in subjection to the governing authorities. For there is no authority except from God, and those which exist are established by God . . . because of this you also pay taxes, for rulers are servants of God, devoting themselves to this very thing. Render to all what is due them: tax to whom tax is due"* (Romans 13:1, 6–7).

It's certainly permissible to reduce taxes by using legal tax deductions, but we should be careful not to make unwise decisions—or deliberately and dishonestly seek to avoid our tax obligations.

CHAPTER SEVEN

Family

Marriage

Creating trust is an indispensabl
healthy marriage. You can't hav~ _ _
riage without great trust.

Each of us has what I call a *Trust Account.* Just as with a bank account, you can make deposits and withdrawals from your spouse's trust account. You make deposits by good communication, honesty, transparency, and seeking to be a blessing to your spouse. Withdrawals are made by dishonesty, lack of financial disclosure, not seeking your spouse's advice, and not wanting to be a blessing to your mate.

There are no shortcuts to filling your spouse's trust account. Trust must be earned, and once violated, it often takes a long time to recover. It's not enough for the offender to confess. True repentance means turning from and changing direction, and it is confirmed only by action— consistent action over a long period of time.

Dare I say, "Years"?

Sexual Dishonesty

Dishonesty destroys and alienates close relationships. This is most vividly experienced in marriage when one of the spouses violates the marriage vow (a covenant to limit sex to each other) d is unfaithful, resulting in deep hurt and a crushing sense of betrayal. Your spouse should be your most intimate ally as you navigate life together. But when trust is broken and lies cover it up, it is extraordinarily painful.

"If two of you on earth agree about anything they ask for, it will be done for them by my Father in heaven. For where two or three gather in my name, there I am with them."
(Matthew 18:19–20).

The Modesto Manifesto

By 1948, Billy Graham was becoming well known as an evangelist, and was receiving more and more invitations to hold city-wide evangelistic meetings. To many, however, evangelists had a bad reputation because of misdeeds on the part of some earlier evangelists.

During his crusades in Modesto, California, Graham met with his leadership team to discuss the most common criticisms and how they could be above reproach. The Modesto Manifesto was the name they gave among themselves to the principles they decided to apply from that point on.

They committed to exercise extreme care to avoid even the appearance of any sexual impropriety by never being alone with any woman other than their wife or family member. Graham even refused to allow a nurse to come into his hospital room alone while in his 90s! I made the same commitment to my wife.

Yes, it's been inconvenient at times.

Yes, it's been uncomfortable explaining the reason for this commitment.

Yes, it's been effective.

Yes, we encourage wives to reciprocate by never being alone with any man other than their husband or family members.

Covenant with Your Eyes

When Job was defending his integrity, he said, *"I have made a covenant with my eyes not to look lustfully at a young woman"* (Job 31:1, NIV). This is a standard every man needs to adopt because:

- What we gaze upon becomes what we think about.

- What we think about becomes what we act upon.

A friend shared with me that in less than a week after making this covenant with his eyes, he and his wife attended a social event. As they were leaving, his wife said, "I don't know what's happened to you, but I'm so much more secure in our marriage since you stopped staring at other women." He had no clue that she had noticed this pattern in life.

The guardrails of never being alone with a person of the opposite sex other than your mate and family members—and making a covenant with your eyes—will go a long way in protecting you from marital infidelity and building an even closer relationship with your spouse.

Financial Dishonesty

Sex may be the first thing that comes to mind when you hear the word "infidelity," but there are other ways spouses are unfaithful and cheat on each other.

Many couples commit monetary deceit in their marriages. Someone lies about finances or doesn't share the details. It can be innocuous, such as fudging on the cost of purchases or hiding a spending decision. Or it could be more significant, such as having a secret credit card or bank account, serious enough to be considered what some relationship experts call "financial infidelity."

Money Dates

To promote transparent communication, I recommend that married couples take a weekly *money date.* This is something you can do at home at the kitchen table, or wherever you choose. Select an appropriate time during the week to focus on your finances by praying together, reviewing your income and spending for the week, and by celebrating the progress the Lord has enabled you to make.

These weekly money dates are vital because they establish the habit of regular financial conversations *when there is no crisis.* Many couples don't begin a conversation about money unless a problem has surfaced and the panic button has already been punched. Tension can reach the boiling point in a hurry when blame and defensiveness take over. That's when it gets personal and hurtful, with a couple screaming at each other instead of working to resolve the problem.

Praying together should be the first agenda item on your money date. I can't emphasize this too much. Jesus makes this remarkable promise in Matthew 18:19–20: *"If two of you on earth agree about anything they ask for, it will be done for them by my Father in heaven. For where two or three gather in my name, there I am with them."*

When a couple prays together about their finances, they learn what is truly important to their mate. What's more, they invite the God of the universe to be personally involved with their earning and spending. How is that for motivation to pray together!

Couples make better decisions when they both understand their true financial situation. The *money dates* are for fact finding only, so establish ground rules together: no nagging, unkind accusations, or angry responses. (And no changing the ground rules in the middle of the date!)

Hard Truths

One of the most sensitive challenges to honesty in marriage can be when a wife asks her husband if he likes her appearance – hair, face, clothes, weight, etc.

The husband realizes that his approval of her appearance is extremely important to her. How should he truthfully respond, for example, when he thinks her dress is unattractive? How can he be a truth teller and an encouragement to his wife?

Here are two suggestions. First, start now on working together to create an environment of love and relentless encouragement in your marriage so that your spouse knows that you *always* want the best for him or her. Often compliment your spouse's appearance, talents, counsel, and anything else worthy of praise.

Dr. Zehngebot was my first wife's oncologist during her five-year journey with cancer. It started with a double mastectomy, then spread to her bones and finally ended in her death. We loved Dr. Zehngebot because he was extraordinarily kind and encouraging. Because we knew he wanted the best for Bev, we were always receptive even when he told us the hard truth about her deteriorating health.

Second, discuss this issue *before* your wife asks these questions. Talk about the wife's need for her husband's approval and the husband's desire not to hurt her feelings. Try to come to agreement on how he should best respond.

Children

In 1904, the country of Wales experienced a remarkable revival. Thousands of people were introduced to Christ, and the results were dramatic. Within a couple of months Wales was a changed nation. Crime was reduced to almost nothing. Often judges were given a ceremonial pair of white gloves when they arrived at the courtroom, signifying that there were no cases to try. Bars closed because of lack of business.[2] Wales was so evangelically-minded that it sent missionaries all over the world.

One of those missionaries traveled to Argentina, where he led a young boy to Christ. The boy's name was Luis Palau. He later became known as the "Billy Graham" of Latin America. In later years, Palau visited Wales to express his thankfulness for the missionaries who led him to Christ. What he discovered was astonishing. Less than one-half of one percent of the Welsh attended church. Divorce was at an all-time high, and crime was increasing. Stone churches stood empty in many villages—or were used as barns to store hay.

As a result of this experience, Palau produced a film titled, *God Has No Grandchildren*. The thrust of the film is that each generation is responsible for passing on the truths of Scripture, including honesty, to its children. Proverbs 22:6 reads, *"Train up a child in the way he should go, even when he is old he will not depart from it."*

Parents have the priceless opportunity to cultivate honest children. The best way to train the next generation is for parents to become MVP parents. MVP is an acronym that describes the three methods to teach children to be honest: *Modeling, Verbal communication,* and *Practical opportunities.* All three are needed, so let's look at each.

Modeling

Since children soak up parental attitudes like sponges soak up water, parents must model honesty and integrity. Paul recognized the importance of modeling when he said, *"Be imitators of me, just as I also am of Christ"* (1 Corinthians 11:1).

Luke 6:40 is a challenging passage. It reads, *". . . Everyone, after he has been fully trained, will be like his teacher."* Another way of saying this is that we can teach what we believe, but we reproduce only who we are. There is no substitute for parents being good models.

When my children were young, if we discovered that we had received too much change after paying a bill, we would return to the store. The kids and I would go in and together reimburse the cashier. This simple act of honesty made an indelible impact that they still remember.

Verbal Communication

Parents also need to tell their children *why* they are committed to live honestly by reviewing the Bible passages that deal with honesty. The Lord charged the Israelites, *"These words, which I am commanding you today, shall be on your heart. You shall teach them diligently to your sons* [and daughters] *and shall talk of them when you sit in your house and when you walk by the way and when you lie down and when you rise up"* (Deuteronomy 6:6–7). We must verbally instruct children in the ways of the Lord, but children need more than a good example and verbal instruction; they also need practical experience.

Practical Experience

Provide occasions for your children to apply what they've seen you do and heard you say. The older they become, the greater the opportunities for them practice honesty.

A wise place to start is to create a series of hypothetical questions dealing with honesty for them to answer. For example, what would you do if . . .

- the store clerk gave you back too much change?

- your friend suggested that you tell your parents a lie?

- a classmate suggested that you cheat on an exam?

- you found some money your neighbor lost?

- a classmate wanted to copy your homework?

- your parents regulate the amount of screen time that you are allowed to watch

on your devices, and you know you've
already exceeded the set time?

- a friend invites you to shoplift some toys
at the store?

When children are old enough, encourage them
to work for others by babysitting, mowing lawns,
or other appropriate jobs. If they learn how to work
hard and honestly, they will have taken a giant step
toward becoming a valuable employee or leader.

Grandparents

Grandparents can play an irreplaceable role with
their grandchildren. Usually they are the most
important influence, after the parents, on their
grandchildren.

We recommend that the parents meet with
the grandparents and together design a strategy
for training the children to become honest individuals. It's important for grandparents to play
a role in which they complement and reinforce
the objectives of the parents. Too often parents
and grandparents have not reached agreement on
how to train the next generation. This can lead to
bruised relationships and ineffective training.

Become an MVP parent or grandparent and
provide the younger generation an inheritance, a
gift that will last their lifetimes—the heritage of
integrity and character.

CHAPTER EIGHT

Honesty – in the Church

Although rare, some of the most tragic cases of dishonesty are in the church. For example, the leadership uses the church funds for their own personal benefit without disclosure to the congregation. A church leader enters into an adulterous affair with a member and tries to hide it. A member sells a fraudulent investment to other church members after promising a safe, highly profitable return.

Too often people have had their faith in Christ damaged or even destroyed when there is dishonesty in the church.

Christ responded in anger to His discovery of dishonesty in the temple. *"Jesus entered the temple and drove out all those who were buying and selling in the temple, and overturned the tables of the money-changers and the seats of those who were selling doves. And He said to them, 'It is written, "My house shall be called a house of prayer;" but you are making it a robbers' den'"* (Matthew 21:12-13).

Two chapters later, Jesus warned the religious leaders, *"Woe to you, scribes and Pharisees, hypocrites! For you clean the outside of the cup and of the dish, but inside they are full of robbery and self-indulgence"* (Matthew 23:25). Those must have been shocking words for those proud, self-righteous leaders to hear. Who had ever dared to speak to them in such a way? It was strong medicine, but Jesus knew that nothing less would do in that confrontation.

In the early church, the Lord dealt with dishonesty even more severely. *"... Ananias, with his wife Sapphira, sold a piece of property, and kept back some of the price for himself, with his wife's full knowledge, and bringing a portion of it, he laid it at the apostles' feet. But Peter said, 'Ananias, why has Satan filled your heart to lie to the Holy Spirit ... **You have not lied to men, but to God.**' And as he heard these words, Ananias fell down and breathed his last ...*

"[later] Peter said to [Sapphira], 'Why is it that you have agreed together to put the Spirit of the Lord to the test? Behold, the feet of those who have buried your husband are at the door, and they will carry you out as well.' And she fell immediately at his feet and breathed her last ..." (Acts 5:1–10, emphasis added).

Carefully review this remarkable passage. A married couple sold property and conspired to lie to Peter by misrepresenting the sales price. Peter, however, perceived that Satan was the origin of their falsehood.

Peter also recognized something else. Even through it seemed that Ananias and Sapphira were only lying to him, in reality they were lying to God Himself. This is a classic example of how dishonesty not only damages our relationship with people, but even more tragically, damages the intimacy of our relationship with the Lord.

Choosing Church Leaders

Church leaders must be chosen on the basis of proven character and conduct, including honesty.

- *"Deacons are to be worthy of respect, sincere . . . **not pursuing dishonest gain**"* (1 Timothy 3:8, NIV, emphasis added).

- *"Since an overseer* [church leader] *is entrusted with God's work, he must be blameless – not overbearing, not quick-tempered, not driven to drunkenness, not violent, **not pursuing dishonest gain**. Rather he must be hospitable, one who loves what is good, who is self-controlled, upright, holy and disciplined"* (Titus 1:7–8, NIV, emphasis added).

- *"To the elders among you . . . Be shepherds of God's flock that is under your care, serving as overseers – not because you must, but because you are willing, as God wants you to be; **not greedy for money** . . ."* (1 Peter 5:1–2, NIV, emphasis added).

Financial Accountability and Transparency

One of the keys to overcome the temptation to misappropriate church offerings is so obvious it shouldn't need to be mentioned.

But I will mention it anyway.

Several respected individuals from the congregation need to be involved in processing these funds. The task should never be assigned exclusively to the pastor, his family or close friends. The Apostle Paul is an example of inviting this accountability.

"*And we are sending along with* [Titus] *the brother who is praised by all the churches . . . to accompany us as we carry the offering, which we administer in order to honor the Lord himself and to show our eagerness to help. We want to avoid any criticism of the way we administer this liberal gift. **For we are taking pains to do what is right, not only in the eyes of the Lord but also in the eyes of man**"* (2 Corinthians 8:18–21, NIV, emphasis added).

Don't skim over Paul's words: *"we are taking pains to do what is right, not only in the eyes of the Lord but also in the eyes of man."* The fact is, people today have the same questions and suspicions that people had 2,000 years ago. And they deserve the same assurances.

It is also wise for church leaders to communicate regularly how money is spent and the financial condition of the church—income, expenses, the amount of debt, and cash in the bank. Accountability and transparency provide church members the confidence that money is being handled wisely and with integrity. This gives them more trust in the leadership, and they tend to become even more generous.

Sexual Guardrails

A gifted pastor started a church in his home with ten people, and overtime it became large and influential.

Then, the unthinkable happened. He became sexually involved with a younger woman at church. As you might imagine, the repercussions were horrendous. It was like a bomb exploding in the congregation, sending sharp pieces of shrapnel far into the community. An emotional divorce ensued after 40 years of marriage. Their children chose sides and now refuse to communicate with one another. The church suffered, and the pastor's Christian testimony in the community was shattered.

He experienced what God warns will happen when people are deceitful, especially those who violate the covenant and promises made when married: *"No one who hopes in you* [Lord] *will ever be put to shame, **but shame will come on those who are treacherous without cause.** Show me your ways, Lord, teach me your paths. Guide me in your truth and teach me, for you are God my Savior"* (Psalm 25:3–5, NIV).

One of this pastor's church leaders observed, "Position and fame can be dangerous attractions to the opposite sex."

It is imperative for the pastor and church leaders to be vigilant and proactive to protect themselves from infidelity. This can be accomplished by constructing the same three guardrails we addressed in the Family Chapter:

- Avoid even the appearance of any sexual impropriety by *never* being alone with the opposite sex other than your spouse or family member. Yes, it will be awkward at times, but so what? The benefits far outweigh the potential for disaster.

- Enter into a Covenant with your eyes. *"I have made a covenant with my eyes not to look lustfully at a young woman"* (Job 31:1, NIV).

- Invite accountability with a person of integrity who will regularly ask you, "Are you emotionally attracted to anyone other than your spouse?"

"We want to avoid any criticism of the way we administer this liberal gift. For we are taking pains to do what is right, not only in the eyes of the Lord but also in the eyes of man"
(2 Corinthians 8:18–21, NIV).

Caution Ahead! – Wolves in Sheep's Clothing

All too often investment scams target and prey upon church members. The perpetrator often is a member of the church, and sets out to exploit the inherent trust within the church. Oftentimes, the person will try to enlist the help of a church leader to market the investment scheme. In this case, the leader becomes an unwitting pawn in the fraudulent scheme.

If you are exposed to an investment opportunity at church that seems too good to be true, more often than not, it *will* be too good to be true.

CHAPTER NINE

Honesty in Work

Despite what many believe, God hardwired us to work.

Work was initiated for our benefit in the sinless environment of the Garden of Eden; it's not a result of the curse! *"The LORD God took the man and put him into the garden of Eden to cultivate it and keep it"* (Genesis 2:15).

The very first thing the Lord did with Adam was to put him to work.

After the Fall, however, everything changed. When sin infected the human race, work became more difficult. *". . . Cursed is the ground because of you; in toil you will eat of it all the days of your life. Both thorns and thistles it shall grow for you; and you will eat the plants of the field; by the sweat of your face you will eat bread . . ."* (Genesis 3:17–19).

Work is so important that God gives us this command in Exodus 34:21: *"You shall work six days . . ."* The Apostle Paul is just as direct: *". . . If anyone is not willing to work, then he is not to eat"* (2 Thessalonians 3:10). Examine the verse carefully. It says, *"If anyone is not **willing** to work."* It does not say, *"If anyone **cannot** work."* This principle does not apply to those who are physically or mentally unable to work; it is for those who are able but choose not to work.

The Lord intends our work to develop our character. While a carpenter is building a house, the house is also building the carpenter. His skills, diligence, integrity, and judgment are refined. A job isn't merely designed to earn money; it is also intended to produce godly character, including a commitment to honesty in the life of the worker.

The Bible treats all types of honest work with equal dignity. The Scripture does not elevate any profession above another; we find in its pages a wide variety of vocations. David was a shepherd and a king. Lydia was a retailer who sold purple fabric. Daniel was a government worker. Mary was a homemaker. Paul operated a tent-making business. And the Lord Jesus Himself was a carpenter.

Our Work Is Our Pulpit

God strategically places His children everywhere. Many believe that only the missionary or pastor is truly spiritual, but this isn't true. In his book, *God Owns My Business*, Stanley Tam writes, "Although I believe in the application of good principles in business, I place far more confidence in the conviction that I have a call from God. I am convinced that His purpose for me is in the business world. **My business is my pulpit**."[3]

The working person is in a position to influence people for Christ who would rarely consider attending a church. When I worked in real estate development, I felt as if I was just as much in full-time ministry as a missionary. A friend told me that followers of Christ involved with secular work should be considered "marketplace clergy." We often have a better opportunity to reach people for Christ in the marketplace rubbing shoulders with them five days a week than most pastors have in just one day a week.

To take advantage of this opportunity, it is essential that we model honesty. We serve a God who commands us, *"Be holy yourselves also in all your behavior; because it is written, 'You shall be holy, for I am holy* (1 Peter 1:15-16). And our Savior, Jesus Christ, described himself as *"the way, and **the truth** and the life . . ."* (John 14:6, NIV, emphasis added).

One of the quickest and most devastating ways to destroy our credibility among those with whom we work is hypocrisy—saying one thing but living a very different life. Far more valuable than anything we might gain by dishonesty are the people who might reject Christ because of our duplicity. As we've seen earlier, Paul said, *". . . prove yourselves to be blameless and innocent, children of God above reproach in the midst of a crooked*

*and perverse generation, among whom you appear as
lights in the world"* (Philippians 2:15).

"Although I believe in the
application of good principles
in business, I place far more
confidence in the conviction
that I have a call from God. I am
convinced that His purpose for
me is in the business world. My
business is my pulpit."

— Stanley Tam

Called to Secular Work

Robert Gilmour "R.G." LeTourneau was 14
years old when he dropped out of the sixth
grade. A decade later, he and his wife were
broke, and heavily in debt from a failed
automobile dealership.

His sister, a missionary, challenged him to
make a real difference for Christ. LeTourneau
was confused and felt guilty because he thought
that he would have to become a missionary and

give up what he really wanted to do—move dirt. Finally, he yielded his will to the Lord and prayed, "Lord, if You'll help me, I'll do anything You want me to do." LeTourneau knew his prayer was answered, because he was overcome with joy.

The very next day, to seal his commitment, he met with his pastor to seek direction. After praying together for some time, the pastor finally said, "R.G., the Lord needs preachers and missionaries, but God needs businesspeople, too."

LeTourneau was stunned. If God needed businessmen, he could easily find a better one than a dirt mover buried under a mountain of debt. Finally, he reasoned, *Well, if that's what God wants me to be, I'll be His businessman.* From that day on, he was in business with God.

LeTourneau's early efforts at tinkering with earth-moving machinery uncovered a knack for innovation. He started manufacturing heavy construction machinery, and the company became enormously successful. In 1935, at the suggestion of his wife, they decided to give 90 percent of the company's profits to the Lord. LeTourneau explained this decision: "It's not how much of *my* money I give to God, but how much of *God's* money I keep for myself."

During World War II, his company built 70 percent of all the earth-moving equipment used by the Allies. He registered more than 300 patents, and there isn't a piece of heavy construction equipment manufactured today that did not find its origin on R.G. LeTourneau's drafting table.[4]

So, if you work, there is one question you must answer.

Don't rush to answer it. Take your time to carefully consider it.

If God wants me to serve Him in my work, am I willing to be His honest worker?

God's Role in Work and Business

How many times have we heard stories of individuals pulling themselves up by their bootstraps and becoming proud, self-made men or women of achievement? It's certainly true that a successful career usually requires great personal effort, but Scripture reveals that God plays the most important role.

Understanding God's role should be a significant factor in our pursuit of honesty in work. Consider these principles from God's Word.

God gives us the ability to make wealth. *"He* [the Lord] *gave you manna to eat in the desert, something* *your fathers had never known, to humble and to test you so that in the end it might go well with you. You may say to yourself, 'My power and the strength of my hands have produced this wealth for me.'* **But remember the** Lord **your God, for it is he who gives you the ability to produce wealth"** (Deuteronomy 8:16–18, NIV, emphasis added).

God controls our promotion. Psalm 75:6–7 reads, *"For promotion and power come from nowhere on earth, but only from God"* (TLB). As much as it may surprise people, their boss is not the one who controls whether they will be promoted. It is the Lord alone who promotes.

God gives us our success. The life of Joseph is a perfect example of God working behind the scene to accomplish His purpose by elevating a person. *"The Lord was with Joseph, so he became a successful man. . . . his master saw that the Lord was with him and how the Lord caused all that he did to prosper in his hand"* (Genesis 39:2–3).

God teaches us to profit. *"Thus says the Lord, your Redeemer, the Holy One of Israel, 'I am the Lord your God, who teaches you to profit, who leads you in the way you should go'"* (Isaiah 48:17).

God gives us our skills. Exodus 36:1 illustrates this truth: *". . . and every skillful person in whom the Lord has put skill and understanding to know how to perform all the work . . ."* God has given each of us unique skills. People have widely varied abilities, manual skills, intellectual capacities, and sometimes hidden reservoirs of giftedness. It's not a matter of one person being better than another; it's simply a matter of having received different abilities.

The true story of God's role in work stands in stark contrast to the assumptions of our culture. Most people believe that they alone are responsible for their job skills, financial success, and promotions. This flawed perspective more easily leads to dishonesty.

Those with a biblical understanding, however, approach this with an entirely different frame of reference. For a few minutes, reflect on God's role. He is the owner of everything you have ever had or ever will have. He gives you your skills, controls any success or promotions you may experience, opens doors of opportunity for you (that you could have never opened for yourself) and provides you with necessary creativity and abilities.

Our Role in Work and Business

And what does God require from us in work? It isn't rocket science. He wants us to be faithful diligent workers. *"Whatever your hand finds to do, do it with all your might"* (Ecclesiastes 9:10, NIV). ".

. . The precious possession of a man [and woman] *is diligence"* (Proverbs 12:27). And He strongly condemns laziness. *"He also who is slack in his work is brother to him who destroys"* (Proverbs 18:9).

As we have repeatedly discovered throughout this book, the Lord also wants His followers to be completely honest. And where does it start? What sets our feet on an honest path? It begins when we focus on obedience instead of compromise; commitment instead of convenience. It is doing what is right rather than what is expedient.

It requires faith and courage to be honest in your work or business because of the challenges of competition, taxes, difficult regulations, meeting payroll and overhead expenses, and an uncertain and changing economy. On top of that, far too many colleagues at work, customers, vendors, and competitors believe the lie: "It's dog-eat-dog out there! You can't be honest and succeed."

In Hebrews Chapter 11, we find "faith's Hall of Fame." Sixteen people are commended for their faith, and only Samuel was a religious professional. All the rest were people in the marketplace who experienced some of the same basic challenges you and I face most every day.

Internal Controls in Business

Employee frauds are often perpetrated by first-time offenders who believe they will avoid detection because of the lack of adequate internal controls. They think to themselves, *I can get away with this, so why not? It will never come to light.* If the proper checks and balances exist, it becomes much more difficult to defraud an organization.

It's obvious that good internal controls protect the organization. But that's not all. They also protect the employees. Without these safeguards, an employee may more easily be tempted.

When Rick Boxx started his banking career, his first position was in the fraud department.

Margie was an exceptionally capable and efficient employee in one of their branch banks. Her manager kept piling on new responsibilities because of her outstanding performance and *can-do* attitude. Eventually, Margie became solely responsible for the certified checks department. She received the deposits, drafted and distributed the checks, and reconciled the monthly balances.

Everything was good until an emergency hit Margie's only son. The immediate cash needed to resolve his crisis was more than Margie could afford. Since she was the only employee working in the certified checks department, she decided to embezzle the funds and repay them as soon as she received her next paycheck.

Unfortunately, her son's crisis became more acute, requiring even more financial support. She continued to embezzle funds over the next several months. Margie was hooked! Once her son's problem was solved, she continued to steal – but on an even grander scale.

A minor illness forced her to stay home for two days, and during her brief absence, a certified checked bounced. While searching for the cause of the overdraft, the bank discovered Margie's theft.

After Rick Boxx and the fraud department confirmed the embezzlement, they, along with the FBI, confronted Margie. She confessed and was sent to prison.

Upon her release, her former branch bank manager helped her secure a job outside the bank. In answer to why he felt compelled to assist Margie, he explained, "I did not protect her by having adequate internal controls in place. If I had, it would have made it impossible for her to begin embezzling. To really care for our staff, we must implement and maintain adequate controls."[5]

CHAPTER TEN

Blessings and Curses

When it comes to acting with honesty or dishonesty, God has left the choice up to us. He has given us clear principles and guidelines—as well as strong commands—to help us choose wisely. As the prophet Micah reminds us, *"He has told you, O man* [and woman], *what is good"* (Micah 6:8). When we find ourselves at the crossroads of honesty or dishonesty, He essentially says, "You choose."

Every such decision, however, comes with consequences. When a person chooses to be dishonest, there may be some short-term benefits—which are all-too-often followed by long-term adversities.

Honesty doesn't always operate under the *Law of Pinocchio,* the fairytale character whose nose instantly grew whenever he lied. Rather, it usually operates under the *Law of the Harvest.* Farmers sow seeds now and reap crops later, sometimes much later.

When people are dishonest, *"they sow the wind and they reap the whirlwind"* (Hosea 8:7). In His timing, because of His great love for us, the Lord will discipline the dishonest with the objective of changing us into people of integrity.

Listed below are some of the blessings the Lord has promised for the honest, and some of the curses reserved for the dishonest. Read these slowly and prayerfully. Meditate on them. Ask God to use these passages to motivate you to a life of complete honesty.

Blessings for the Honest

Blessing of a more intimate relationship with the Lord

"O LORD, who may abide in Your tent? Who may dwell on Your holy hill? He who walks with integrity, and works righteousness, and speaks truth in his heart" (Psalm 15:1–2).

"Lying lips are an abomination to the LORD, but those who deal faithfully are His delight" (Proverbs 12:22).

Blessing of protection and provision

". . . He [the Lord] is a shield to those who walk in integrity" (Proverbs 2:7).

"He who walks righteously, and . . . he who rejects unjust gain . . . his refuge will be the impregnable rock; his bread will be given him, his water will be sure" (Isaiah 33:15–16).

Blessing on the family

"A righteous man who walks in his integrity – how blessed are his sons [and daughters] after him" (Proverbs 20:7).

Blessing of life

"Whoever of you loves life and desires to see many good days, keep your tongue from evil and your lips from telling lies" (Psalm 34:12-13, NIV).

"Truthful lips will be established forever, but a lying tongue is only for a moment" (Proverbs 12:19).

Blessing of the respect of others

"Do not let kindness and truth leave you . . . So you will find favor and good repute in the sight of God and man" (Proverbs 3:3-4).

Blessing of prosperity

"Great wealth is in the house of the righteous, but trouble is in the income of the wicked" (Proverbs 15:6).

Curses Reserved for the Dishonest

Curse of alienation from God

"There are six things which the Lord hates, yes, seven which are an abomination to Him: . . . a lying tongue . . . a false witness who utters lies . . ." (Proverbs 6:16-19).

Curse on the family

"He who profits illicitly troubles his own house, but he who hates bribes will live" (Proverbs 15:27).

Curse of destruction and death

"A worthless person, a wicked man, is the one who walks with a false mouth . . . his calamity will come suddenly; instantly he will be broken, and there will be no healing" (Proverbs 6:12, 15).

"The acquisition of treasures by a lying tongue is a fleeting vapor, the pursuit of death" (Proverbs 21:6).

Curse on possessions

"Wealth obtained by fraud dwindles" (Proverbs 13:11).

> *"Lying lips are an abomination to the Lord, but those who deal faithfully are His delight"*
> (Proverbs 12:22)

Nations

It's a simple fact of life that many nations in today's world have a pervasive culture of deeply ingrained dishonesty. The government, businesses, average income earners, and sometimes even the religious community embrace and practice dishonesty. Many of these nations have historically struggled with widespread chronic poverty.

The prophet Jeremiah lived in such a country and described the serious consequences. "'... *lies and not truth prevail in the land* [of Judah]; *for they proceed from evil to evil, and they do not know Me,'* declares the LORD. ... 'everyone deceives his neighbor and does not speak the truth, they have taught their tongue to speak lies ... it speaks deceit; with his mouth one speaks peace to his neighbor, but inwardly he sets an ambush for him.* **Shall I not punish them for these things?'* declares the** Lord. **'On a nation such as this shall I not avenge Myself?'**" (Jeremiah 9:3–9, emphasis added).

The population of Judah had not understood that the Lord requires and is pleased by truth. He intended it to be an indispensable part of the glue that would hold the country together. Without it there would be no basis for the citizens to trust one another and the country's institutions. Worse, the Lord would not bless such a nation until a healthy percentage of its citizens become honest people of integrity.

Here are some questions for you to answer:

1. How would you describe the general culture of your country: honest or dishonest?

2. Is the population in your country becoming more honest or dishonest?

3. How can you encourage your countrymen and women to become people of integrity?

CHAPTER ELEVEN

What We Do Now Matters Forever

On Monday, October 25, 1999, the news reported an unfolding story. Air Force jets following a Learjet from Orlando, Florida, were unable to communicate with its pilots. I learned later that two of my friends, Robert Fraley and Van Ardan, were on that Learjet as it carried them and professional golfer Payne Stewart to their deaths.

Life is short and eternity is long; it never ends. What we do during our lifetime matters to God. This should be a key motivation for us to be honest. Robert and Van, in their mid-forties, lived with an eternal perspective. Robert had framed these words of Saint Augustine in his workout area: "Take care of your body as though you will live forever; take care of your soul as though you will die tomorrow."

When the Lord reveals in the Scriptures that there is a heaven and a hell, that there is a coming judgment, and that He will grant eternal rewards unequally, God does this because He loves us. The Lord wants to motivate us to invest our lives in such a way that we can enjoy an intimate relationship with Him now, and the greatest possible rewards in heaven.

Scripture exhorts us again and again to allow the certainty of our eternal future to influence our life on earth. Those who don't know the Lord, however, look at life as beginning at birth and ending at death. They tell themselves, *If this life is all there is, why not do anything I want? What does it really matter?*

Those who know Christ understand that this life on earth is brief. It's the trailer, not the movie. James 4:4 describes it this way, *"You are just a vapor that appears for a little while and then vanishes away."* And I can assure you from personal experience—the older you become, it seems the faster it goes! Even so, this brief period will determine much of our experience in heaven *throughout eternity.*

Financial planners try to persuade clients to look down the road instead of simply focusing on today. "Think and plan for 30 years from now" they will advise you. The wise person does indeed think ahead, but far more than 30 years ahead—more like *30 million* years ahead. Second Corinthians 4:18 says it this way: *"So we fix our eyes not on what is seen, but on what is unseen, since what is seen is temporary, but what is unseen is eternal"* (NIV).

The Long and Short of It

The Bible frequently reminds us that life on earth is brief: "[God] *is mindful that we are but dust"* (Psalm 103:14). David sought to gain God's perspective on the brevity of life. He asked of the

Lord, *"Show me, O LORD, my life's end and the number of my days; let me know how fleeting is my life . . . Each man's life is but a breath"* (Psalm 39:4–5). In his 90s, evangelist Billy Graham observed, "The greatest surprise of my life, is the brevity of life."

Moses realized that true wisdom requires an awareness of the brevity of our lives, so he asked the Lord to help him number the days he had on earth. *"As for the days of our life, they contain seventy years, or if due to strength, eighty years . . . for soon it is gone and we fly away. So, teach us to number our days, that we may present to You a heart of wisdom"* (Psalm 90:10, 12).

Moses had a good idea there.

I encourage you to actually number the estimated days you have left on earth. Does that strike you as morbid? It isn't! In fact, it brings every day of your life into sharper relief and clarity. It reminds you that there is no such thing as a throw-away day. It's also a valuable reminder that you are one day closer to heaven!

If I live as long as the average of my father and mother, as of today I have about 3,500 days left. And they will go by fast! This has helped me zero in on investing my life to please the Lord. In light of the brevity of life, Matthew Henry said, "It ought to be the business of every day to prepare for our last day."

Eternity Is Long

Eternity, on the other hand, *never ends.* It is for-ever. Imagine a cable running through the room where you are now. To your right, the cable runs billions of light years, all the way to the end of the universe; to your left, it runs to the other end of the universe. Now imagine that the cable to your left represents eternity past, and the cable to your right, eternity future. Imagine taking out a marker and making a tiny line on the cable in front of you. That tiny mark represents your brief life on earth.

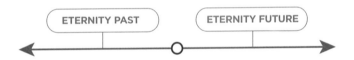

Most people live their lives as if the mark was everything. They make *mark* choices, drive *mark* cars, raise *mark* children, and dream *mark* dreams. Devotional writer A. W. Tozer referred to eternity as "the long tomorrow." This is the backdrop against which all the questions of life should be answered and our decisions made.

Judgment

It's uncomfortable to think about judgment. However, because our Lord loves us deeply, He wants us to realize what will happen in the future. For this reason, God revealed to us that we all will be judged according to our actions. *"Nothing in all creation is hidden from God's sight. Everything is uncovered and laid bare before the eyes of him to whom we must give account"* (Hebrews 4:13, NIV). *"God will bring every deed into judgment, including every hidden thing, whether it is good or evil"* (Ecclesiastes 12:14, NIV).

The Bible teaches that all those who do not know Christ will be judged and sent to an unspeakably horrible destiny. *"I saw a great white throne and him who was seated on it. . . . And I saw the dead, great and small, standing before the throne . . . Each person was judged according to what they had done. . . . Anyone whose name was not found written in the book of life was thrown into the lake of fire"* (Revelation 20:11–15, NIV).

You Can Know God

Realizing that we can know God personally changes everything! I was 28 years old when I started meeting with several young business-men. It wasn't long before I was impressed by their business savvy. But more than that, I was attracted to their integrity. I didn't know what they had, but whatever it was, I wanted it.

These men spoke openly of their faith in God. I had grown up going to church, but the religion

I had seen modeled during those years meant nothing to me as an adult. I had concluded it was only a fairy tale—until a friend described how I could enter into a *personal* relationship with Jesus Christ. He explained several truths from the Bible I had never understood before.

God Knows You Personally

The following passages are but a small sample of how personally the Lord is involved in your life:

- *God wrote every day of your life in His book before you were born.* "*Your eyes saw my unformed body; all the days ordained for me were written in your book before one of them came to be. How precious to me are your thoughts, God! How vast is the sum of them! Were I to count them, they would outnumber the grains of sand . . .*" (Psalm 139:16–18, NIV).

- *God is constantly with you.* "*You have searched me, LORD, and you know me. You know when I sit and when I rise; you perceive my thoughts from afar. You discern my going out and my lying down; you are familiar with all my ways. Before a word is on my tongue you, Lord, know it completely*" (Psalm 139:1–4, NIV).

All your life you have been on a treasure hunt. You've been searching for a perfect person and perfect place. Jesus is that person and heaven is that place.

—Randy Alcorn

God Wants You to Know Him Personally

God desires a close relationship with each of us. *"For God so loved the world, that He gave His only begotten Son, that whoever believes in Him shall not perish, but have eternal life"* (John 3:16). *". . . I [Jesus] came that they may have life, and have it abundantly"* (John 10:10).

It is crucial for you to recognize how extravagantly God loves you. Perhaps this example will help you understand the depth of His love. In the 1992 Olympics in Barcelona, Spain, Great Britain had a runner named Derek Redmond whose lifelong dream had been winning the gold medal in the 400-meter race. As the gun sounded for the semifinals, Derek knew he was running the race of his life. Then tragically, as he entered the backstretch, Redmond felt pain shoot up the back of his right leg. A torn hamstring sent him sprawling face down on the track.

Instinctively, Derek struggled to his feet in excruciating pain and began hopping on one leg toward the finish line. Suddenly a large man came bounding from the stands. Flinging aside security guards, he made his way onto the field and threw his arms around Derek. It was Jim Redmond, Derek's father. "Son, you don't have to do this," he said.

"Yes, Dad, I do," Derek answered.

"All right then, let's finish this together," said the older man. And that's exactly what they did. With the son's head frequently buried in the father's shoulder, they made it to the end of the race as the crowd rose to its feet, weeping and cheering![6]

Derek Redmond didn't win an Olympic gold medal that day. He didn't get the silver or bronze, either. But he won something far more valuable. He walked away from the race with the memory of a father who was not only in the stands cheering, but who loved him too much to watch him suffer from a distance—a father who came down out of the stands and entered the race with him, staying beside him every step of the way.[7]

We have a heavenly Father who watches us with eyes of love. He is our Father-God who cared for us too deeply to stay in heaven, looking down on us, watching us fall and fail. Instead, He came down out of the stands and into our race in the person of His Son, Jesus Christ. And He is committed to staying in this race with us until we have safely crossed the finish line.[8]

Unfortunately, we are separated from God.

God is holy, which simply means He is perfect and can't have a relationship with anyone who is not perfect. My friend asked if I had ever sinned—done anything that would disqualify me from perfection. "Many times," I admitted. He explained that every person has sinned, and the consequence of sin is separation from God. *"All have sinned and fall short of the glory of God"* (Romans 3:23).

The Gap Between God and Humanity

People (SINFUL)

God (HOLY)

God's only provision to bridge this gap is Jesus Christ.

Jesus Christ died on the cross to pay the penalty for our sin, bridging the gap between God and us. Jesus said, *"I am the way, and the truth, and the life; no one comes to the Father but through Me"* (John 14:6). *"God demonstrates His own love toward us, in that while we were yet sinners, Christ died for us"* (Romans 5:8).

This personal relationship is a gift from God.

My friend explained that by faith I could receive the free gift of a personal relationship with God. *"It is by grace you have been saved, through faith—and this is not from yourselves, it is the gift of God—not by works, so that no one can boast"* (Ephesians 2:8-9, NIV).

I had only to ask Jesus Christ to come into my life to be my Savior and Lord. So I did! As my friends will tell you, I'm a very practical person; if something doesn't work, I stop doing it. I can tell you from more than 45 years of experience that a relationship with God is real. And it is available to you only through Jesus Christ. Nothing in life—and I literally mean *nothing*—compares with knowing Christ personally. You can experience true peace, joy, and hope when you know Him. It's the only way you can enjoy a truly meaningful life and leave an eternally significant legacy.

If you want to know God and are not certain whether you have this relationship, I encourage you to receive Jesus Christ right now. Pray a prayer similar to the one I prayed: "God, I need You. I'm sorry for my sin. I invite Jesus to come into my life as my Savior and Lord, and to make me the person You want me to be. Thank You for forgiving my sins and giving me the gift of eternal life."

If you asked Christ into your life, you have made the most important decision anyone could ever make. *". . . God has given us eternal life, and this life is in his Son. Whoever has the Son has life; whoever does not have the Son of God does not have life. I write these things to you who believe in the name of the Son of God so that you may know that you have eternal life"* (1 John 5:11–13, NIV).

I urge you to find a church that teaches the Bible, one where you can begin to learn what it means to follow Jesus Christ.

Judgment of Believers

After they die, those who know Christ will spend eternity with the Lord in heaven, an indescribably magnificent place. The entry point to heaven, however, is a judgment.

Scripture teaches that all believers in Christ will give an account of their lives to the Lord. *". . . We will all stand before the judgment seat of God. So then each one of us will give an account of himself to God"* (Romans 14:10, 12). The result of this will be the gain or loss of eternal rewards. In 1 Corinthians 3:13–15, we read, *"Their work will be shown for what it is, because the* [Judgment] *Day will bring it to light. . . . If what has been built survives, the builder will receive a reward. If it is burned up, the builder will suffer loss"* (NIV). Part of what we are judged on is honest or dishonest behavior.

God's Word doesn't treat this judgment as just a meaningless formality. Not at all! Scripture presents it as an epic event in which things of eternal significance are brought to light.

Motivation and Rewards

The prospect of eternal rewards for our honesty is a key to unlocking our motivation. Our daily choices are of eternal importance.

In his outstanding book, *Money, Possessions and Eternity*, Randy Alcorn tells the story of Alfred Nobel. Nobel was a Swedish chemist who made his fortune by inventing powerful explosives, which were bought by governments to produce weapons. When Nobel's brother died, one newspaper accidentally printed Alfred's obituary. He was described as a man who became rich by enabling people to kill each other on a massive scale. Shaken by this assessment, Nobel resolved to use his fortune to reward accomplishments that benefited humanity, resulting in what we now know as the Nobel Peace Prize.

Let us put ourselves in Nobel's place. Let us read our own obituary, not as written by uninformed people, but as it would be written from heaven's point of view. Then let us use the rest of our lives to edit that obituary into what we really want it to be.[9]

I loved playing Little League baseball as a young boy. We played on a huge field with towering fences in the outfield. Years later, shortly after my father died, I spent the day walking around my old hometown, reflecting on his life.

When I visited the baseball field, I was shocked! It was so small! I could actually step over the outfield fences. While standing there, a thought struck me: *Many of those things that seem so large and important to us today shrink to insignificance in just a few years.*

When I am face-to-face with Christ and look back on my life, I want to see that the things in which I invested my time, influence, and money are big things to Him. I don't want to squander my life on things that won't matter throughout eternity. What matters the most in the end, matters most now.

What choices regarding honesty challenge you now? How does an eternal perspective influence your decisions? Martin Luther said his calendar consisted of only two days: "today" and "that Day." May we invest all that we are and have today in light of *that* day.

CHAPTER TWELVE

FINISHING WELL

When it comes to finishing well, there's good news and bad news. The good news is that there are unforgettable biblical examples of those who crossed life's finish line with courage and their commitment to God firmly intact.

Jesus finished well. In John 17:4 Jesus prayed to His Father, *"I have brought you glory on earth by completing the work you gave me to do"* (John 17:4, NIV).

The Apostle Paul finished well. The Holy Spirit had revealed to him that traveling to Jerusalem meant prison and hardships. His response? *"I consider my life worth nothing to me, if only I may finish the race and complete the task the Lord Jesus has given me"* (Acts 20:24, NIV, emphasis added).

But here's the problem; most people don't. When people used to ask evangelist Billy Graham how they could pray for him, he invariably responded, "Pray that I finish my life well and don't dishonor the Lord." He recognized how rare it is for people to remain faithful to the Lord to the end.

According to Dr. Howard Hendricks, of the 2,930 individuals mentioned in the Bible, we know significant details about only 100 of them. Of those 100, only about one-third finished well.

Of the two-thirds who did not finish well, most failed in the second half of their lives.

In your journey with the Lord and in dealing with honesty, it's not how you start that matters; it's how you finish. What are you doing to become the one in three who reaches the finish line still serving Christ with integrity? You will need to be intentional and exercise spiritual discipline to have a strong finishing kick when you hit the tape at age 65, 75, 85, or whatever age God calls you home.

The Christian life isn't a 100-yard dash; it's a marathon. Long races don't require speed; they require grit, determination, and commitment. You see, it's endurance that determines whether a person will finish strong. And endurance is the byproduct of godly character, especially when it comes to honesty.

As Scripture says, *"Therefore, since we have so great a cloud of witnesses surrounding us, let us also lay aside every encumbrance and the sin which so easily entangles us, and let us run with endurance the race that is set before us, fixing our eyes on Jesus"* (Hebrews 12:1-2).

Don't Give Up!

Finishing well doesn't mean finishing with a perfect record of honesty. But it does mean learning from our mistakes, getting back on course, and pursuing honesty with our whole heart. We are to be diligent in pursuing a closer relationship with Jesus Christ and in applying the truths of the Bible—despite any previous mistakes we may have made.

As you read these words, you may think it's already too late for you to finish well. Perhaps you've made some big, dishonest, bone-headed mistakes. Many of those who finished well in the Bible were guilty of terrible decisions. Abraham lied. Moses committed murder. David was an adulterer and a murderer. Peter denied Christ three times.

Paul, the murderous persecutor of the early church, said it this way: *"... One thing I do: forgetting what lies behind and reaching forward to what lies ahead, I press on toward the goal for the prize of the upward call of God in Christ Jesus"* (Philippians 3:13–14).

We Need to Practice!

Just as a sports team practices to become better, practice is required for Christian growth. As the Apostle Paul instructed Timothy, *"... train yourself to be godly"* (1 Timothy 4:8, NIV) The key habits for finishing well and maintaining integrity are Bible reading, prayer, serving others, and having a close relationship based on trust, confidentiality, and accountability with at least one or two other followers of Christ.

"Go up and down the streets of Jerusalem, look around and consider, search through her squares. If you can find but one person who deals honestly and seeks the truth, I will forgive this city."
(Jeremiah 5:1, NIV).

Bible Reading

No spiritual practice is more important than spending time reading or listening to God's Word. There is no such thing as a vibrant Christian life apart from it. In the Bible, God reveals Himself. Only in the Scriptures do we find how to live in a way that pleases God and is, as a by-product, the most fulfilling for us.

When Jesus asked people about their understanding of the Scriptures, He often began with the words, "Have you not read?" He assumed that those claiming to be the people of God would have read the Word of God. Unfortunately, this is often not the case.

When Jesus said, *"Man shall not live on bread alone, but on every word that proceeds out of the mouth of God"* (Matthew 4:4), surely, He intended for us to read every word. Too often, we tend to read Old Testament accounts merely as biblical history without relating them to our lives. However, Romans 15:4 says, *"For everything that was written in the past was written to teach us, so that through endurance and the **encouragement of the Scriptures** we might have hope"* (NIV, emphasis added). These stories, principles and commands are meant to encourage us and teach us truth that we can apply to our circumstances.

The Bible makes these remarkable claims about itself: *"The word of God is living and active and sharper than any two-edged sword . . . and able to judge the thoughts and intentions of the heart"* (Hebrews 4:12). *"All Scripture is God-breathed and is useful for teaching, rebuking, correcting and training in righteousness, so that the man* [and woman] *of God may be thoroughly equipped for every good work"* (2 Timothy 3:16-17, NIV). Since the Bible is living and God-breathed, shouldn't we read and study it?

Here are suggestions for consistent success in Bible reading.

Find the time. Perhaps one of the main reasons Christians never read through the entire Bible is its length. But do you realize that tape-recorded readings of the Bible have proved that you can read through the entire Bible in about 70 hours? In no more than 15 minutes a day you can read through the Bible in a year's time. Try to make it the same time every day.

Find a Bible-reading plan. It's no wonder that those who simply open the Bible at random each day soon drop the practice. There are effective Bible-reading plans available, and some Bibles are designed to read through in a year. One of the best is *The Daily Walk Bible.*

Find a Bible study. Most of us will be more consistent if we become involved in a Bible study. We need the encouragement and accountability of a group. And one of the greatest benefits of a group is the development of close relationships with others who are seeking to know the Lord better.

Prayer

If prayer could have been unnecessary for anyone, it would have been the sinless Son of God, Jesus Christ. However, it was one of His most consistent practices. *"Jesus often withdrew to lonely places and prayed"* (Luke 5:16, NIV).

He prayed before the critical events in His life. "*. . . Jesus went out to a mountainside to pray, and spent the night praying to God. When morning came, he called his disciples to him and chose twelve of them, whom he also designated apostles*" (Luke 6:12–13, NIV).

Even in the midst of His busy public ministry, the Lord consistently spent time alone with His Heavenly Father. Jesus is our ultimate example for prayer.[10]

Fundamental to intimacy with the Lord is honesty in our prayer lives. As C. S. Lewis said, we should "lay before Him what is in us, not what ought to be in us." The Father is pleased that you are willing to come to Him as His child and spend time with Him, so come as naturally as you can.

As with reading the Bible, most of us will be more consistent if we establish a regular time in our daily schedule to pray. It is also helpful to establish a list of people and circumstances for which to pray.

Benefits of Finishing Well

Many people imagine that following Christ and committing to be a completely honest person will be a boring experience—with long faces and endless lists of things you cannot do. Nothing could be further from the truth. The Lord is dynamic, and He intends for us to live vibrant, fulfilling lives. Jesus said it this way in John 10:10, *"I came that they may have life, and have it abundantly."*

My prayer is that you would finish well so that you will hear these words from the Lord ringing in your ears throughout eternity, *"Well done, good and faithful servant. . . . Enter into the joy of your master"* (Matthew 25:21, ESV).

In addition to these priceless words, I encourage you to meditate on this promise from Christ: *"To him who overcomes* [finishes well], *I will give the right to sit with me on my throne, just as I overcame* [finished well], *and sat down with my Father on his throne"* (Revelation 3:21, NIV).

Stop for a moment!

Please think about this.

Imagine how you would feel to be invited by Jesus Christ to sit with Him on His heavenly throne. Nothing on earth that you might gain by being dishonest will ever come close to that experience.

Will You Be that One Honest Person?

In the first chapter, we explored how rare honesty is and how important it is to God. Remember what Jeremiah 5:1 tells us, *"Go up and down the streets of Jerusalem, look around and consider, search through her squares. If you can find **but one person who deals honestly and seeks the truth,** I will forgive this city"* (NIV, emphasis added).

The future of the city hung in the balance, and what was the Lord looking for before judging it? Just one honest person.

Let me ask you again: Are you willing to be that one person in your family, work, or community? If you are that person, you will please the Lord Jesus Christ.

So, learn from your past mistakes. Be courageous. Stay focused on Christ. Invite the Holy Spirit to live through you. Never abandon your commitment to be an absolutely honest follower of Jesus.

Endnotes

[1] *Business God's Way*, Compass – Finances God's Way, Howard Dayton. The names and type of organization have been changed in the story.

[2] Evan Roberts & the Welsh Revival (spiritofgrace.org)

[3] Stanley Tam, *God Owns My Business*, Harvest House Publishers.

[4] R.G. LeTourneau, *Movers of Men and Mountains*, Moody Publishers 2009

[5] Rick Boxx, *Unconventional Business Network*, Visit unconventionalbusiness.org

[6] Derek Redmond story, Visit derekredmond.com

[7] Farrar, Steve. *Finishing Strong*. Colorado Springs: Multnomah Books, 2000.

[8] Cloninger, Claire, *Dear Abba*. Nashville: Thomas Nelson, 1997.

[9] Randy Alcorn, *Money, Possessions and Eternity*, Randy Alcorn, (Wheaton, IL: Tyndale House Publishers, 1989, 2003).

[10] J. Oswald Sanders, *Spiritual Leadership*, Moody Publishers, 1986, 2007.

The Compass – *finances God's way*™
Vision, Mission & Values

Our Vision

To see everyone, everywhere faithfully living by God's financial principles in every area of their lives.

Our Mission

Equipping people worldwide to faithfully apply God's financial principles so they may know Christ more intimately, be free to serve Him and help fund the Great Commission.

Core Values

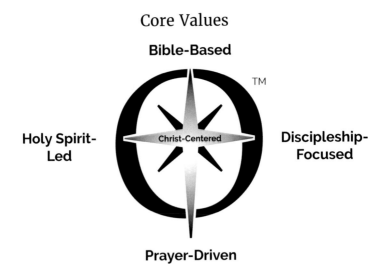

Bible-Based

Holy Spirit-Led

Christ-Centered

Discipleship-Focused

Prayer-Driven

Continue The Journey...

Congratulations on completing *Honesty: A missing key to unlocking intimacy with God*. We hope the Lord has had a significant impact on your financial discipleship journey through this book.

The financial discipleship journey is one that doesn't end until we hear the words *"well done, good and faithful servant."* We encourage you to continue on this journey in one of two ways.

Continue your journey by engaging in studies, tools, and resources that will help you grow. Visit us at **ContinueGrowing.org** to learn more.

Continue your journey by paying it forward and helping others grow. To learn more, visit us at **HelpOthersGrow.org**.

Thank you for the time and effort you have invested in this book. We pray the Lord will draw you ever nearer to Him as you continue to grow and help others grow.

About the Author

HOWARD DAYTON is the founder of Compass–finances God's way and cofounder of Crown Financial Ministries. Serving as an unpaid fulltime volunteer at both organizations, Howard also hosted the nationally syndicated radio program MoneyWise. His books and small group studies have been translated into dozens of languages and are used by millions of individuals.

A former naval officer and graduate of Cornell University, Howard's business career was developing office buildings in the Orlando, Florida area. His life radically changed in 1971 when Jesus Christ became his savior. Searching for financial wisdom, he and his partner discovered 2,350 verses in the Bible dealing with money and possessions.

Howard's passion to share the Bible's life–changing principles led him to write eight books and seven small group studies, including Your Money Counts, Money and Marriage God's Way, Business God's Way and Charting Your Legacy. He collaborated with the American Bible Society in the production of The Financial Stewardship Bible.

Howard holds an honorary doctorate from Asbury University. Asbury's Howard Dayton School of Business was renamed the Howard and Beverly Dayton School of Business to honor his wife of 46 years after she died from cancer.

In 2019, Howard married Lynn. Residing in Orlando, Florida, their family includes five adult children and nine wonderful grandchildren.

Compass – *Finances God's Way*™
compass1.org · 407-331-6000